W9-BZJ-137

WORLD SOCCER LEGENDS

# ALEX MORGAN

## SECOND EDITION

**Abbeville Press Publishers**
New York · London

A portion of this book's proceeds are donated to the **Hugo Bustamante AYSO Playership Fund**, a national scholarship program to help ensure that no child misses the chance to play AYSO Soccer. Donations to the fund cover the cost of registration and a uniform for a child in need.

**Text by** Illugi Jökulsson
**Design:** Ólafur Gunnar Guðlaugsson
**Layout:** Ólafur Gunnar Guðlaugsson and Árni Torfason

**For Abbeville Press**
**Project Editors:** David Fabricant and Lauren Bucca
**Copy Editor:** Elisha Aaron
**Layout:** Ada Rodriguez
**Production Manager:** Louise Kurtz

**PHOTOGRAPHY CREDITS**

**Getty Images:** p. 8 Berlin Wall (Pool CHUTE DUMUR BERLIN/Gamma-Rapho), p. 9 Maradona (Michael King), p. 12 (Topical Press Agency), p. 13 Marta (Popperfoto), p. 13 Wen (Lars Baron/Bongarts), p. 13 Prinz (Lutz Bongarts/Bongarts), p. 15 (Robert Beck/Sports Illustrated), p. 16 Lilly (Elsa), p. 16 Akers (Aubrey Washington/Allsport), p. 17 (George Tiedemann/Sports Illustrated), p. 19 (Mike Zarrilli), p. 22 (Alexandra Beier-FIFA), p. 21 and back cover bottom (Jonathan Ferrey), p. 23 (Kevin C. Cox-FIFA), p. 25 (Stanley Chou), p. 27 (Ronald Martinez), p. 29 (Ronald Martinez), p. 33 (Kevin Mazur/Fox), pp. 36–37 and back cover bottom (Celso Junior), p. 41 (Jesse Grant), p. 53 (Catherine Ivill-FIFA), p. 58 (Brian Ach/WireImage), p. 60 (Kamee June Photography), pp. 62–63 (Ira L. Black/Corbis)

**Shutterstock:** front cover (feelphoto), pp. 2–3 (twobee), pp. 6–7 (feelphoto), pp. 10–11 background (trekandshoot), p. 11 inset (Mat Hayward), p. 31 (lev radin), p. 34 (Jose Breton-Pics Action), p. 35 (Jose Breton-Pics Action), p. 39 (Jaguar PS), p. 42 (feelphoto), p. 43 (Jose Breton-Pics Action), p. 44 Ertz (Jose Breton-Pics Action), p. 44 Mewis (feelphoto), p. 44 Lavelle (feelphoto), p. 45 Sauerbrunn (Jose Breton-Pics Action), p. 45 Dahlkemper (Romain Biard), p. 46 O'Hara (Romain Biard), p. 46 Dunn (Jose Breton-Pics Action), p. 46 Naeher (Jose Breton-Pics Action), p. 46 Horan (feelphoto), p. 47 Pugh (Leonard Zhukovsky), p. 47 Lloyd (Romain Biard), p. 47 Heath (Romain Biard), p. 47 Press (Romain Biard), p. 48 and back cover top (feelphoto), p. 49 (feelphoto), pp. 50–51 (Jose Breton-Pics Action), p. 54 (Romain Biard), pp. 56–57 and back cover middle (Jose Breton-Pics Action), p. 61 (Featureflash Photo Agency)

**Wikimedia Commons:** p. 15 Fawcett (Johnmaxmena2, CC-SA-3.0), p. 15 Foudy (RyanDowIMG)

This edition first published in the United States of America in 2020 by Abbeville Press, 655 Third Avenue, New York, NY 10017

Second Edition
10 9 8 7 6 5 4 3 2 1

*A previous edition of this book was cataloged as follows:*
Library of Congress Cataloging-in-Publication Data
Ilugi Jökulsson
[Alex Morgan. English]
Alex Morgan / Illlugi Jvkulsson.
Pages cm. — (World soccer legends)
Summary: "Recounts the story of American soccer star Alex Morgan, one of the best female players in the world. The book tracks her success in helping to win the FIFA World Cup, a team gold medal in the 2012 Olympics, and her achievements outside of soccer, including writing and modeling" — Provided by publisher.
ISBN 978-0-7892-1216-0 (hardback)
1. Morgan, Alex (Alexandra Patricia), 1989—Juvenile literature. 2. Women soccer players—United States—Biography—Juvenile literature. I. Title.
GV942.7.M67315513 2015
796.334092—dc23
[B]
2014045290

For bulk and premium sales and for text adoption procedures, write to Customer Service Manager, Abbeville Press, 655 Third Avenue, New York, NY 10017, or call 1-800-ARTBOOK.

Visit Abbeville Press online at www.abbeville.com.

# CONTENTS

# ALEX

Alexandra Patricia Morgan Carrasco is one of the most outstanding American athletes of the twenty-first century. She has been instrumental in helping the US women's soccer team win two World Cups and an Olympic gold medal. Morgan enjoyed many sports growing up and only began to focus on soccer when she was fourteen years old—rather late for someone of her caliber. Yet her speed, agility, and resolute attacking spirit catapulted her immediately to the top. Morgan is a superb athlete both on and off the field: she is an unyielding fighter in the most positive sense of the term, and she places great emphasis on being a strong role model for young people. Her leadership is always an inspiration as she dashes across the field with a cheerful yet determined expression on her face, on the hunt for goal-scoring chances as well as passes to her teammates. When she is not accumulating accolades, you can find her training hard or engaged in her various side projects, such as writing soccer-themed novels or promoting a healthier lifestyle. From early on, Morgan learned to follow the example of her athletic idols. Now she is the idol to countless young soccer players across the United States, and even around the world.

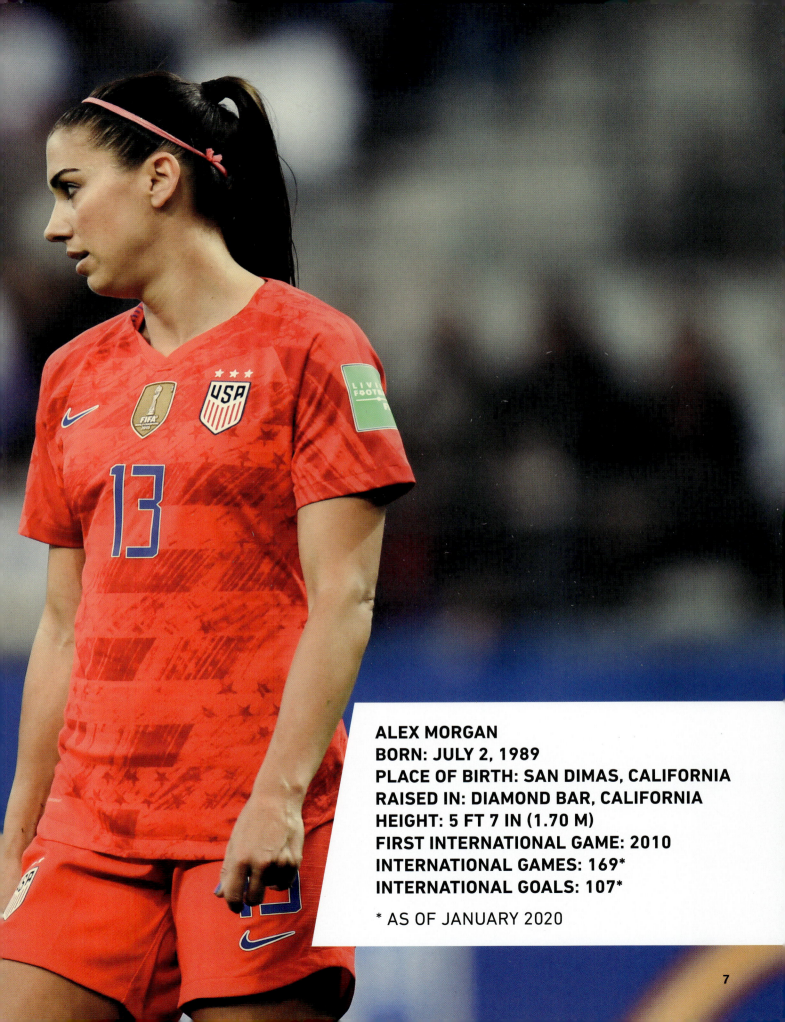

ALEX MORGAN
BORN: JULY 2, 1989
PLACE OF BIRTH: SAN DIMAS, CALIFORNIA
RAISED IN: DIAMOND BAR, CALIFORNIA
HEIGHT: 5 FT 7 IN (1.70 M)
FIRST INTERNATIONAL GAME: 2010
INTERNATIONAL GAMES: 169*
INTERNATIONAL GOALS: 107*

* AS OF JANUARY 2020

# THE YEAR SHE WAS BORN: 1989

**What happened in 1989?**
When Morgan was born in July, US president George H. W. Bush had been in office for six months after succeeding Ronald Reagan.

In June, the student protests in Tiananmen Square in Beijing came to a tragic end when Chinese government troops killed thousands of unarmed protesters. Positive events took place, too: the oppressive communist regimes of central and eastern Europe collapsed in the autumn.

January 20: Bush takes over from Reagan.

November 9: The Berlin Wall comes crumbling down.

## CANCER & SNAKE!

Alex Morgan's zodiac sign is Cancer, according to Western astrology. Individuals born under the Cancer sign are said to be loyal and dependable, especially when it comes to their family, friends, and loved ones. They can also be a bit prone to mood swings!

According to Chinese astrology, Alex was born in the year of the snake. In China, this is not considered negative in any way, because snakes are seen as highly intelligent creatures. Earth is Alex's Chinese element. Her modern birthstone is ruby, and her Zodiac birthstone is emerald.

Note: Astrology can be a lot of fun, but it has no scientific basis.

## Films of the Year

The highest-grossing film of 1989 was the third installment in the Indiana Jones series, *Indiana Jones and the Last Crusade*, starring Harrison Ford and Sean Connery. *Indiana Jones* was followed by *Batman*, played by Michael Keaton, with Jack Nicholson in the role of the

Joker. Other popular films that year were *Back to the Future Part II*, *Look Who's Talking*, *Dead Poet's Society*, and Disney's *The Little Mermaid*.

*Driving Miss Daisy* won the Academy Award for the Best Picture of 1989. *Born on the 4th of July*, directed by Oliver Stone, also received numerous awards.

## MARADONA

Argentina was the reigning world champion in men's soccer after winning the 1986 World Cup in Mexico, led by Diego Maradona.

Costa Rica became CONCACAF (Confederation of North, Central American and Caribbean Association Football) soccer champions in 1989, closely followed by the USA. Both teams qualified for the 1990 FIFA Men's World Cup, the US team qualifying for the first time since 1950.

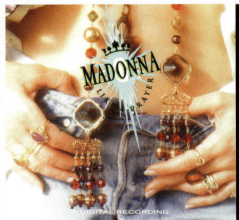

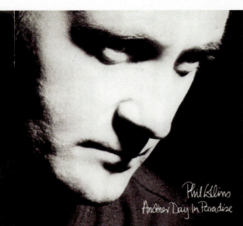

## THE BIGGEST HIT SINGLES OF 1989

1. Madonna: "Like a Prayer"
2. The Bangles: "Eternal Flame"
3. Phil Collins: "Another Day in Paradise"

# GROWING UP IN DIAMOND BAR

Alex Morgan was born in Diamond Bar, California, a city close to Los Angeles. The land on which Diamond Bar stands was once home to a ranch. In 1847, the rancher at the time passed away, and his widow sold the land in exchange for one hundred calves, one hundred dollars in merchandise, and payment of her husband's debts. Farming continued on the land until the 1950s, when a large corporation bought the land in order to develop a residential area. The new city grew quickly and was incorporated in 1989.

The city is named after the "diamond over a bar" branding iron that was registered in 1918 by ranch owner Frederick E. Lewis.

Los Angeles
Diamond Bar

Alex Morgan grew up in the "quiet, sunny and generally happy" suburban community of Diamond Bar. She enjoyed the closeness of the community and was able to walk to elementary and middle school.

As in many small cities, however, there wasn't much going on. "It was a huge deal when we got a Target," Morgan wrote. There were few restaurants and things to do, and most activities revolved around sports. "It's the kind of place that you're happy to grow up in but also happy to get out of" when you come of age, she recalled.

Alex's family was very close and loving. She has two sisters, Jenny and Jeri, who are six and four years older than Alex. Her parents "basically grew up together." Alex's father Michael ran a small construction company (much like the father of Megan Rapinoe, a USWNT teammate), and her mother Pamela worked for him until she decided to get her master's degree in 1995.

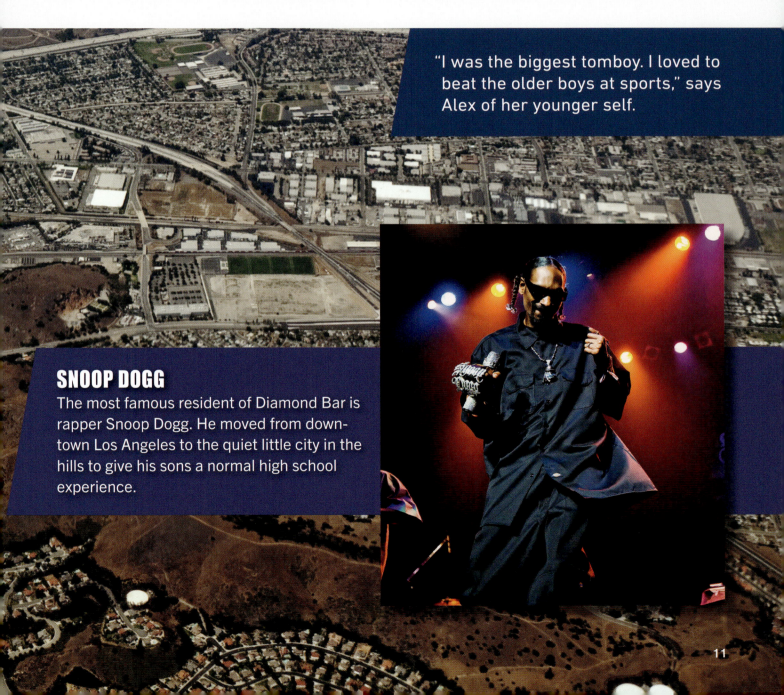

"I was the biggest tomboy. I loved to beat the older boys at sports," says Alex of her younger self.

### SNOOP DOGG

The most famous resident of Diamond Bar is rapper Snoop Dogg. He moved from downtown Los Angeles to the quiet little city in the hills to give his sons a normal high school experience.

# THE RISE OF WOMEN'S SOCCER

These are some of the biggest stars in women's soccer in recent decades from outside of the United States.

A women's game in Britain in 1914. There was no lack of spectators.

Soccer's origins can be traced to nineteenth-century England. Various sports similar to soccer had been played in England for a long time, but they were finally united under the aegis of the British Football Association in 1863. From England the sport spread across the world, with the United States embracing soccer by the end of the century.

It so happened that, a few years earlier, a closely related sport took root in the United States, one that was inspired by British rugby. This sport quickly became very popular in the US and took on the name "football." When the British Football Association's sport later traveled across the Atlantic, it was dubbed "soccer" by the Americans. (The name was taken from the word "asSOCiation.")

Soon after men began playing soccer in Europe, women also took to the field. After the First World War (1914–1918), women's soccer caught on in Britain, and tens of thousands of people came to watch the games. Reacting to the popularity of women's soccer, the male players attempted to stop its progress: women were

forbidden to play on [...] This rule went into eff[...] world as well. Women's [...] cally repressed, and it w[...] soccer was "inappropriat[...] velopment of women's so[...] a halt for decades. Women [...] again in the latter part of the [...] and the popularity of women [...] steadily increased around the world.

In the US, women's soccer received a huge boost when Title IX, a portion of the federal Education Amendments of 1972, was passed. This law stipulated that schools were required to fund athletic programs for males and females equally. Even though attempts to found a women's professional league had gotten off to a rocky start, soccer flourished in schools and colleges. A national team was established, and it played its first game in 1985. From the beginning, Team USA was characterized by a daring fighting spirit, and it quickly entered the list of the world's greatest soccer teams.

**MARTA**
**BRAZIL**
Born 1986
With the Brazilian national team since 2002
Games 151*
Goals 107

FIFA World Player of the Year 2006, 2007, 2008, 2009, 2010 & 2018*

**SUN WEN**
**CHINA**
Born 1973
With the Chinese national team 1990–2006
Games 163
Goals 106

FIFA Female Player of the 20th Century (with Michelle Akers)

**BIRGIT PRINZ**
**GERMANY**
Born 1977
With the German national team 1994–2011
Games 214
Goals 128

FIFA World Player of the Year 2003, 2004 & 2005

* As of January 2020

## FIRST WORLD CUP GOLD

The first FIFA Women's World Cup was held in China in 1991. The US team won all their games, most of them comfortably, including a complete lashing of the German team in a 5–2 victory in the semifinal.

### 1991 WOMEN'S WORLD CUP FINAL
NOVEMBER 30, 1991
TIANHE STADIUM, GUANGHOU, CHINA

## USA – NORWAY
### 2–1

AKERS 20, 78,     MEDALEN 29,

HARVEY
BIEFELD – WERDEN – HAMILTON
HAMM – HIGGINS – FOUDY – LILLY
HEINRICHS – AKERS – JENNINGS

## SECOND WORLD CUP GOLD

The US squad, who had captured the gold at the 1996 Olympics, easily defeated their opponents during the group stage of the World Cup. During the knockout stage, the US team managed to defeat extremely tough opposition (Germany and Brazil) and reached the final against China. This competitive match  was not decided until the very last kick.

### 1999 WOMEN'S WORLD CUP FINAL
JULY 10, 1999
ROSE BOWL, PASADENA, CA

## USA – CHINA
### 0–0 (5–4*)

*AFTER EXTRA TIME AND PENALTIES. OVERBECK, FAWCETT, LILLY, HAMM AND CHASTAIN SCORED. SCURRY SAVED ONE CHINESE PENALTY.

SCURRY
OVERBECK – CHASTAIN – FAWCETT – SOBRERO
AKERS (WHALEN 91) – HAMM – LILLY – FOUDY
PARLOW (MACMILLAN 57) – MILBRETT (VENTURINI 115)

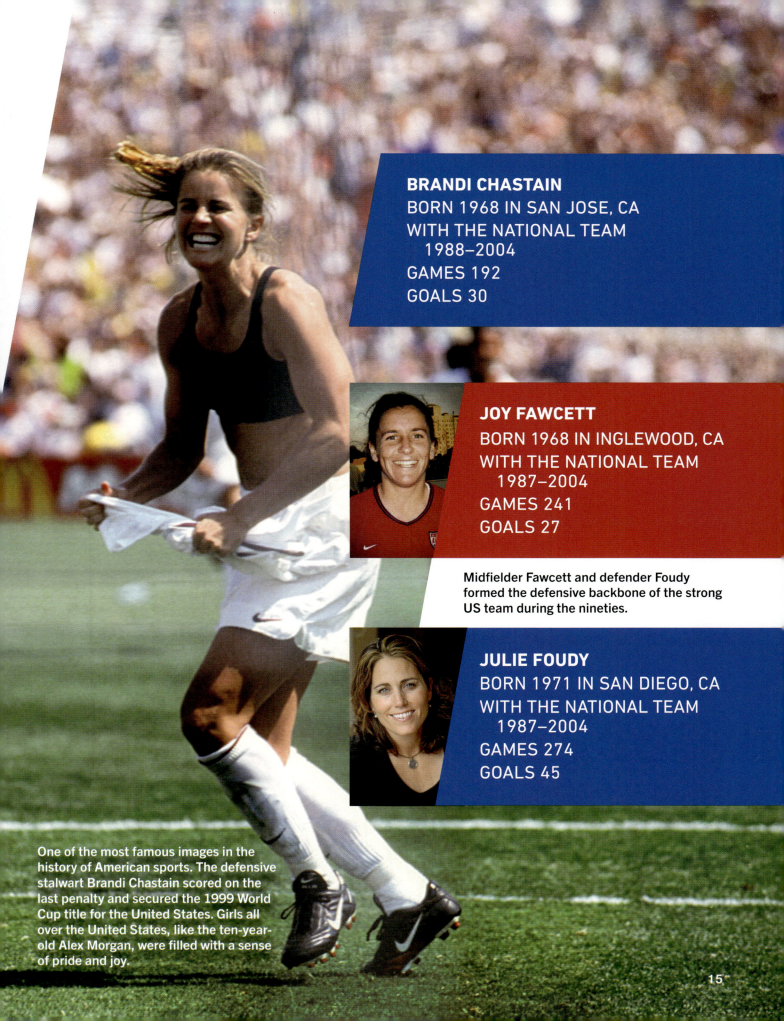

**BRANDI CHASTAIN**
BORN 1968 IN SAN JOSE, CA
WITH THE NATIONAL TEAM
  1988–2004
GAMES 192
GOALS 30

**JOY FAWCETT**
BORN 1968 IN INGLEWOOD, CA
WITH THE NATIONAL TEAM
  1987–2004
GAMES 241
GOALS 27

Midfielder Fawcett and defender Foudy formed the defensive backbone of the strong US team during the nineties.

**JULIE FOUDY**
BORN 1971 IN SAN DIEGO, CA
WITH THE NATIONAL TEAM
  1987–2004
GAMES 274
GOALS 45

One of the most famous images in the history of American sports. The defensive stalwart Brandi Chastain scored on the last penalty and secured the 1999 World Cup title for the United States. Girls all over the United States, like the ten-year-old Alex Morgan, were filled with a sense of pride and joy.

15

# ALEX'S ROLE MODELS

The United States has boasted a number of great women's soccer players. These four dangerous forwards all inspired the young Alex Morgan.

## KRISTINE LILLY
BORN 1971 IN NEW YORK, NY
WITH THE NATIONAL TEAM 1987–2010
GAMES 352
GOALS 130

In a remarkable career, Kristine Lilly won two World Cups and two Olympic gold medals. Lilly is one of only four players—and the sole woman—to have played in five World Cup tournaments. She was an ever-present attacking midfielder on the US team for more than twenty years and she holds the record for most international appearances: a total of 352.

## MICHELLE AKERS
BORN 1966 IN SANTA CLARA, CA
WITH THE NATIONAL TEAM 1985–2000
GAMES 153
GOALS 105

Michelle Akers grew up in Seattle. Tall and athletic, she was an aggressive forward who later changed her position to midfield. She was the top scorer in the first FIFA Women's World Cup in 1991, with a total of ten goals in six games. Akers scored both goals for the US team in the final, securing a 2–1 victory over Norway. She was also a gold medalist at the 1996 Atlanta Olympics.

Akers made an important contribution to the 1999 World Cup winning team and she was included in the tournament's All-Star Team.

In 1999, she was voted FIFA Player of the Century, together with Sun Wen of China.

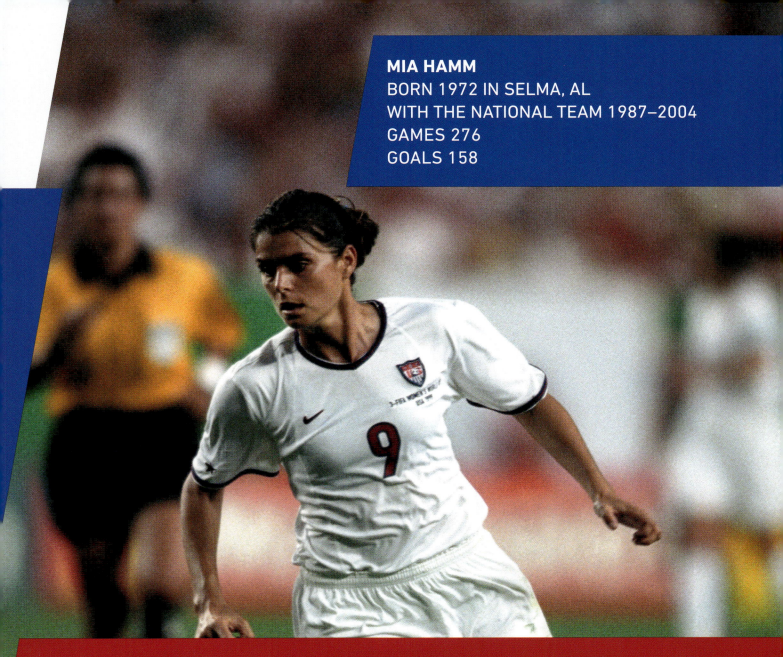

**MIA HAMM**
BORN 1972 IN SELMA, AL
WITH THE NATIONAL TEAM 1987–2004
GAMES 276
GOALS 158

Mia Hamm was introduced to soccer in Italy, where her father was stationed for a time with the US Air Force. Hamm began playing for the national team at fifteen, and is still the youngest woman ever to play for the US national team. An extremely prolific goal scorer, Hamm was a member of the US team that was victorious at the World Cup in both 1991 and 1999. She was also on the All-Star team in 1999. Plus, she became an Olympic champion in 1996 and 2004.

Hamm garnered numerous awards throughout her career and was chosen as the FIFA Female Player of the Year the first two years the award was given, in 2001 and 2002. Mia Hamm and Michelle Akers were the only women on a list of the 125 greatest soccer players in history assembled by the soccer legend Pelé.

# COLLEGE AND CLUB STAR

Alex Morgan attended the University of California, Berkeley, from 2007 to 2010. Despite the demands of playing soccer for her school's team, the California Golden Bears, she graduated a semester early with a degree in political economy. Morgan was the top goal scorer during the time she played with the team and accumulated numerous awards.

Since leaving the Golden Bears, Morgan has played with teams across the United States. In spring 2013, she joined the Portland Thorns, which participated in the newly founded National Women's Soccer League (NWSL) and won the league title for that year. In 2016 she joined Orlando Pride in the NWSL, and in 2017 she was on loan to the French team Lyon, where she won the continental European treble. Everywhere Morgan goes she racks up goals with her speed, agility, and energy—she currently holds 33 career NWSL goals.

| Team | City | Season |
|------|------|--------|
| West Coast FC | Los Angeles | 2008–09 |
| California Storm | Sacramento | 2010 |
| Pali Blues | Los Angeles | 2010 |
| Western New York Flash | Buffalo | 2011 |
| Seattle Sounders Women | Seattle | 2012 |
| Portland Thorns FC | Portland | 2013–2015 |
| Orlando Pride | Orlando | 2016– |
| Lyon (loan) | Lyon, France | 2017 |

Alex Morgan signs a young boy's shirt after the Women's Professional Soccer game between the Atlanta Beat and the Western New York Flash at Kennesaw State University Soccer Stadium in Atlanta on August 6, 2011.

# STAR OF THE U-20 TEAM

The 2008 CONCACAF Women's U-20 Championship turned out to be quite a significant event in the history of the USWNT. A group of talented and promising players took their first steps toward success in the tournament, players who would later become the stars of the national team. Alyssa Naeher guarded the goal, with Meghan Klingenberg, Kelley O'Hara, and Sidney Leroux farther upfield, and the eighteen-year-old Alex Morgan on the frontline. Morgan scored her very first goal, against Cuba, on June 20, and although the US team was defeated by Canada in the final, many soccer fans noticed the promise of the swift and goal-hungry Morgan, eagerly battling in the front.

The 2008 FIFA U-20 Women's World Cup was hosted by Chile in November of the same year, and Morgan was of course present. The US faced France in the first game, and Morgan went toe-to-toe with a number of players she would confront many times over the course of her career: defender Wendie Renard and forwards Eugenie Le Sommer and Marie-Laure Delie. After a long stalemate, Morgan finally broke the ice and scored the opening goal of the game. In the tournament, she scored a total of four goals in six games. In the final on December 7, Morgan scored one of the team's two goals, securing a US victory over North Korea.

Alex Morgan immediately revealed her penchant for high-octane soccer. She usually comes into her own in the intensity of a final—her goal in the 2008 U-20 final was nothing short of spectacular. She collected the ball on the North Korean side, dribbled past four defenders, and blasted a long shot into the corner, with the goalkeeper completely beat.

Morgan's fantastic goal was voted the best goal of the tournament, and subsequently selected as FIFA's second-best goal of the year.

Morgan was also awarded the Bronze Shoe as the tournament's third-highest scorer, as well as the Silver Ball as the second-best player of the tournament, behind Leroux.

## A SNOWY INTERNATIONAL GAME

March 31, 2010, was a milestone day for Alex Morgan. That day, she made her first appearance for the USWNT's senior squad in a friendly game against Mexico, held in Sandy, Utah. Morgan substituted in for Amy Rodriguez in the second half. Despite dominating the game overall, the US only managed to score one goal, delivered by Abby Wambach, who was fast approaching the peak of her career. The most notable thing about the game—aside from Alex Morgan's debut—was the snowfall that blanketed the field. As the US team celebrated Wambach's goal, they threw themselves to the ground and made snow angels. This marked the first time that an American national team played in the snow.

# HER FIRST INTERNATIONAL GOALS

Morgan scored her first goal half a year after her debut on the international stage. It was on October 6, 2010, when she appeared as a substitute in a friendly game against China. The Chinese team had control for a good portion of the game. Toward the end of the match, however, Morgan gathered a pass from Wambach near China's penalty box, sliced through two defenders, and delivered a concise shot into the net. Roughly a month later, the US national team was set to play two games against Italy. The stakes were high: qualification for the 2011 Women's World Cup. The US team had made a terrible blunder at the CONCACAF qualification tournament and there was a real danger of not qualifying for the World Cup—that would be disastrous. The first game took place in the Italian city of Padua on November 20. Deep into stoppage time, the scoreline still lingered at 0–0. The second game could prove a massive challenge. Entering the game in the 86th minute, Morgan saw her chance to shine and come to her team's rescue. Carli Lloyd's long pass found Morgan, who proceeded to poke the ball past the Italian goalkeeper.

The US could now enter the second game with a calmer mind. They won it 1–0 and secured a place at the 2011 World Cup in Germany.

## TO THE WORLD CUP

As the 2011 World Cup opening on June 26 drew closer, the coach of the USWNT, Pia Sundhage, picked Morgan for the team, with her fellow forwards Abby Wambach, Amy Rodriguez, and Lauren Cheney. When the tournament started, Morgan had played nineteen international games and scored seven goals. It was an undeniable honor for the twenty-one-year-old Morgan to play alongside veterans such as Christie Rampone/ Pearce, Hope Solo, and Wambach.

Morgan came on as substitute for Rodriguez in the first game against North Korea. The US won the game 2–0, followed by a 3–0 win over Colombia in which Morgan was not involved. She appeared as a substitute in the third game of the group stage, which the US lost to Sweden. In the quarterfinals, the US defeated Brazil after a dramatic battle, extra time, and a penalty shootout. In the semifinal game against France on July 13, the US team won a rather safe victory, 3–1. Morgan came on as a substitute for Rodriguez and, determined to make her mark, decisively nailed the US's third goal in the match and her first goal in a major tournament. She corralled a beautiful pass from Megan Rapinoe through the French defense, played swiftly into the box, and fired a shot straight past the goalkeeper. The US team had made it to the finals, where the tenacious Japanese awaited them.

Alex Morgan and Abby Wambach celebrate Morgan's first goal during the 2011 Women's World Cup final match against Japan in Frankfurt, Germany, on July 17, 2011.

Alex Morgan of USA celebrates her goal against Japan in the 2011 Women's World Cup final match against Japan.

## FIRST GOAL IN THE FINAL

The 2011 World Cup final was held at the Commerzbank Arena in Frankfurt in front of 49,000 fans. Morgan came on in the second half, after a heavily contested first half; in the 59th minute, she scored. She swept up a long ball from Rapinoe, broke free from a Japanese defender, and launched a beautiful shot into the goal. Japan leveled the score, and the game drifted into extra time. With her characteristic fighting spirit and force, Morgan sent a pass from out of a tight spot for Wambach's thumping header to find the back of the net. It seemed that the US was headed for their third World Cup title, but the Japanese equalized just before the game ended, and after three misses in the penalty shootout, Japan came out victorious. It was a great disappointment, but Alex Morgan had delivered an outstanding performance, proving that she deserved a place among the best.

# THE 2012 OLYMPICS

Only nine years after the young Alex Morgan began playing soccer seriously, she featured in the frontlines of an impeccable American national team—the team that won the gold at the 2012 Summer Olympics in London. The biggest dream of every athlete is standing on the Olympic podium with the national anthem playing and a shiny gold medal proudly hanging from their neck. Morgan achieved that dream.

The USWNT went in determined to avoid a repetition of the 2011 World Cup disaster. Coach Pia Sundhage relied on almost the same lineup, which is not strange, as the usual stalwarts such as Hope Solo, Christie Rampone/Pearce, Carli Lloyd, and Abby Wambach were still at the top of their game. And the younger players Alex Morgan and Megan Rapinoe were quickly rising through the ranks.

The first game in London was truly historic. A great start from the young and very promising French national team seemed to throw the US off balance, and the French grew a 2–0 lead only fourteen minutes into the game. But Team USA never gives up! Wambach reduced the deficit with a header, and then, in the 32nd minute, Solo cleared the ball all the way into France's penalty box, where Morgan lay in wait. Morgan found herself in a tight squeeze with two defenders assailing her from both sides and the French goalkeeper speeding forward to snatch the ball, but she broke free and flicked a beautiful volley over the goalie into the wide-open goal. This goal required a high degree of technical skill, and it proved that Morgan had more up her sleeve than just speed and power.

The game was tied, but the second half belonged to the Americans. Lloyd established the US lead, and Morgan then earned them a win in a spectacular cooperation between the team's young players. A classic Rapinoe long pass found the top left flank, where Tobin Heath collected and crossed the ball to Morgan, who then tapped it into the goal.

## ASSISTING WAMBACH

Following the intense victory over France, the USWNT continued their forward march with their characteristic fighting spirit and skill. The team beat Colombia 3–0 and then North Korea 1–0. The winning goal against North Korea was scored by Wambach. Morgan picked up a long pass from Lauren Cheney and positioned the ball neatly in front of her despite two encroaching defenders. Instead of firing the shot herself, Morgan assisted the approaching Wambach, who blasted a bullet into the net.

Team USA struck again in the quarterfinals against New Zealand. Wambach broke the ice after Morgan tricked a couple of defenders and snuck a devious pass to her veteran idol. Just before the end of the game, Sidney Leroux ensured the win with her second goal.

The team forged confidently ahead to the semifinals, where they confronted their Canadian neighbors to the north.

The US national team had won the gold medal at the two preceding Summer Olympics. At the 2004 Summer Olympics in Athens, they beat Brazil 2–1 in extra time. Most of the 1999 world champions were still part of the team, and here the young Abby Wambach scored the game-winning goal. Then, at the 2008 Summer Olympics in Beijing, the US team once again defeated Brazil in the final, 1–0, with Carli Lloyd scoring the winning goal. (The US team had also clinched the gold medal at the 1996 Summer Olympics in Atlanta, when Shannon MacMillin and Tiffeny Milbrett both scored in a 2–1 victory over China in the final.)

# THE SEMIFINALS

Can there be a more exciting moment for a young soccer player than scoring the winning goal for her country at the Olympics, only moments before the game ends? That's exactly what Alex Morgan did during the Olympic semifinals against Canada on August 6, 2012. And it definitely did not make matters worse that the game took place at the legendary Old Trafford stadium, the home field of Manchester United.

The Canadians played the game of their lives and the magnificent Christine Sinclair proved her strength by scoring a hard-won hat trick. But the US leveled the score each time. Their first goal was delivered straight from a Rapinoe corner kick, and then Rapinoe went for another goal with a thunderous blast from outside the box. Wambach scored the third goal from a penalty kick after a Rapinoe shot had glanced off a Canadian player's arm.

Morgan kept building momentum as the game's tension increased. She erupted into Canada's penalty box but was taken down. She could have thrown herself to the ground and called a penalty, but Alex Morgan never quits, and instead drove an elegant pass to the wide-open Wambach. Sadly, her shot flew past the goal.

The game dragged into heavily contested extra time, and both teams intensified their attacks. A powered-up Morgan hunted for the golden chance and received a dangerous pass in the 115th minute, but a foul was called at the last moment. Two minutes later, Morgan sent a riveting cross toward the goal that just barely missed US fielder Heather O'Reilly in the box.

In the 119th minute, Morgan dodged three defenders and reached the byline, but was immediately smothered by Canadian defenders, out of Wambach's reach. Free again, Morgan sent a difficult cross to a hovering Wambach, who headed the ball into the crossbar.

123 minutes into the game, with 30 seconds to go, an O'Reilly cross arrived from the right flank into Canada's box, where Morgan climbed high to arch a powerful header into the top right corner despite a courageous effort by the Canadian goalkeeper.

A devastating heartbreak for Canada but what a performance from Team USA and Alex Morgan!

# FIRST PRIZE

The 2012 Olympic final was held at the famous Wembley Stadium in London. The US's opponents were none other than the Japanese world champions, and the USWNT was hell-bent on winning the game, not only to bring home the gold medal but also to avenge the defeat at the 2011 World Cup. The game turned into a fierce battle. The US dominated but the Japanese showed great endurance, and

took plenty of risky chances. "Morgan's tireless running bought the team so much time," a *Guardian* sports writer said. And Morgan made the assist for the opening goal early in the 8th minute. Tobin Heath fed a low pass to Morgan who burst into the box, turned cleverly and crossed for Lloyd who headed the ball into the back of the net. Lloyd then went on to secure the win with a beautiful individual goal. A fully deserved team victory.

# ALEX'S IDOL

Before the SheBelieves Cup match against England on March 2, 2019, in Nashville, Tennessee, the US Women's National Team decided to honor powerful, influential, iconic, and inspirational women. Each member of the team chose the name of a woman who had inspired her, and wore that woman's name on the back of her jersey during the game. Morgan's teammates drew from a diverse range of women as inspiration. Tierna Davidson chose to honor the first female astronaut, Sally Ride. Crystal Dunn wore legendary tennis player Serena Williams's name on her jersey. Carli Lloyd was inspired by Malala Yousafzai, the Nobel Prize—winning activist for women's education.

Morgan said she wanted to choose someone who had been an inspiration both in her career and in her private life. Even though her mind jumped to famous figures like Michelle Obama and Billie Jean King, she preferred to choose someone she knew. Icons like Obama and King are easy to look up to, said Morgan, but they hadn't necessarily had the biggest impact on her life. Rather, the people who had affected her personally were her family and her teammates.

"There's no one who has helped guide me or [given] me advice and confidence more than Abby," said Morgan. Their partnership was unique; Wambach inspired her belief in herself, and instilled confidence in her, in the most difficult of times. She was always present for Morgan, as a teammate and a friend, despite battling for the same position on the USWNT. In a situation where some might become inward and selfish, Wambach remained supportive and kind. She wanted Morgan to have success, but in Morgan's words, Wambach also "outwardly told me that she wanted me to have more success than she ever had. She wanted me to break whatever records she set." Wambach's support and encouragement were admirable, and helped Morgan in so many ways. And that's why Morgan wore Wambach's name on the back of her jersey.

**ABBY ON ALEX:**
"Watching Alex grow on the field and off has been one of the pleasures of my career."

Abby Wambach and Alex Morgan celebrate their 5—2 win over Japan in the 2015 Women's World Cup final in Vancouver on July 5, 2015.

**ABBY WAMBACH**
BORN 1980 IN ROCHESTER, NY
WITH THE NATIONAL TEAM 2001–2015
GAMES 256
GOALS 184

# ALEX MORGAN, AUTHOR

Alex Morgan was propelled to national stardom following her remarkable performance at the 2012 Olympics; in fact, she became well known around the world. And she had plenty of energy to engage in other projects alongside soccer. Morgan signed with Simon & Schuster in 2012 to write The Kicks, an ongoing book series intended for middle schoolers. The series revolves around four young girls who play soccer, with central themes of friendship, leadership, and loyalty. Morgan said that her aim with the books was to "inspire young girls" and "celebrate" her love of soccer.

Morgan's first novel, *Saving the Team*, was released on May 14, 2013, and she followed it up with a sequel called *Sabotage Season*. More books would follow: *Win or Lose*, *Hat Trick*, *Shaken Up*, and *Settle the Score*, to name a few.

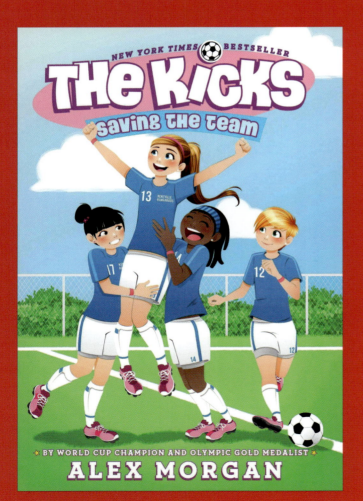

## THE KICKS ON TV

Morgan's books about the adventures of the Kentville Kangaroos became widely popular—even spawning a TV series based on the novels.

In the show, twelve-year-old soccer player Devin Burke (played by Sixx Orange) has her heart set on becoming the captain of her school soccer team in Connecticut, when her family suddenly decides to move to California. Her new school's team has been on a cold streak for a number of months and is in dire need of a dynamic captain to raise their morale and lead them to victory. Devin steps to the fore, but her plans are upset when the team's coach quits. With two important games on the horizon and no coach, the girls recruit the school's janitor, a man named Pablo Rivas, to help them. Rivas is tough but also kindhearted, because he remembers the ups and downs of being a schoolkid their age.

In 2015, Alex Morgan published her autobiography, *Breakaway: Beyond the Goal*, coauthored with Sarah Durand. In the book, Morgan describes her life; her goals and the means she used to achieve them; and her family, friends, teammates, and rivals.

# HER FAVORITE THINGS

## HOBBIES

Writing, paddleboarding, exercise, and spending time with family and friends.

## MOTTO

"I'm just all about female power."

## COLOR

Pink

## FAVORITE FOOD

Morgan, who is fully fluent in Spanish, loves Mexican food. However, she has been exclusively vegan in recent years. Morgan was named one of PETA's Most Beautiful Vegan Celebrities of 2019, together with Kyrie Irving. Speaking to Reuters, Morgan claimed that she decided to become a vegan "because it didn't feel fair to have a dog I adore, and yet eat meat all the time."

## NICKNAME

As a young and aspiring soccer player, Morgan was sometimes called "baby horse" because of how fast she ran. As her career advanced, she outgrew the nickname and, according to Megan Rapinoe, developed into a "full-on stallion."

## FUN FACT

Morgan has a motorcycle license.

## ANIMALS

Morgan loves all animals, cats and dogs in particular. She once had a cat named Brooklyn that had six toes on each of its front paws. Unfortunately, Brooklyn was run over by a car.

## FAVORITE BOOK

*To Kill a Mockingbird* by Harper Lee
*A Thousand Splendid Suns* by Khaled Hosseini

## FAVORITE MOVIES

*Catch Me If You Can*
*The Blind Side*

## MUSIC IDOLS

Beyoncé
Taylor Swift
Katy Perry
Rihanna

## SOME FAVORITE SONGS

"Run the Word (Girls)," Beyoncé
"Man in the Mirror," Michael Jackson
"I Kissed a Girl," Katy Perry
"Can't Hold Us," Macklemore & Ryan Lewis
    feat. Ray Dalton
"Where Have You Been," Rihanna
"Your Song," Ellie Goulding
    (written by Elton John)

## FAVORITE TV SHOW

*Modern Family*

Alex Morgan and Taylor Swift attend the 2019 Teen Choice Awards 2019 in Hermosa Beach, California, on August 11, 2019.

**FAVORITE NUMBER**

13

**FAVORITE *GAMES OF THRONES* CHARACTER**

Daenerys

**HER MOST PRODUCTIVE YEAR**

In 2012, Morgan scored 28 goals and made 21 assists for the USWNT. She was only the second US player to manage at least 20 goals and 20 assists in one calendar year. The first was Mia Hamm, in 1998.

# THE 2015 WORLD CUP

Alex Morgan earned her third world championship title when the USWNT won the 2015 Women's World Cup in Canada. The tournament was held in June and July in six locations, from Vancouver on the west coast to Moncton on the east. The team was coached by the British-born Jill Ellis, who had been appointed to the job the year before.

Morgan was recovering from an injury and came on as a substitute in the first two games, but was placed in the starting lineup in the last game of the group stage.

The team properly came into its own during the knockout stage. Early in the first half of the first match, against Colombia, Morgan was brutally taken down, and Wambach missed the penalty kick. But Morgan would settle the score a few minutes later, when she drilled home a shot from a difficult angle. The US won the game 2–0.

The goal was Morgan's only one at the tournament, but she still tirelessly contributed in every way she could. The US defeated China 1–0 in the quarterfinals and then went up against the German powerhouse in the semifinals. According to the FIFA World Rankings list, Germany ranked number one at the time. Morgan fired an excellent shot in the game that was, however, saved by the German goalkeeper. She was later taken down, whereupon Lloyd stepped up to score on a penalty kick.

An incredible start to the final in Vancouver on July 5 removed all excitement from the match against Japan. In just sixteen minutes, the US grew into a 4–0 lead thanks to a hat trick by the unstoppable Carli Lloyd, who scored one of her goals with a shot from midfield. To give credit where it is due, Japan fought hard, and the game ended with a 5–2 victory for the US.

Alex Morgan and her teammates celebrated the world championship title, also cheering the fact that they had now reached the same summit once occupied by their idols of the 1999 generation.

Carli Lloyd is a fantastic example of how some soccer players only get better with age. She scored the winning goal of the 2008 Summer Olympics and then scored both goals in a 2–1 victory in the 2012 final. She was the top goal scorer (along with Célia Šašić from Germany) at the 2015 World Cup, and she was still in top form at the 2019 World Cup, scoring three goals. By November 2019, the thirty-seven-year-old Lloyd had scored 16 World Cup and Olympic goals.

# A SHOCKER IN RIO

Following the 2015 World Cup victory in Canada, the national team's performance at the 2016 Summer Olympics in Rio proved a major disappointment. The US team had won three consecutive gold medals, but something went astray and they ultimately fell short of their fourth.

Everything had gone according to plan during the group stage, where the US had beaten New Zealand 2–0 (with Morgan scoring one goal) and France 1–0, and then had a 2–2 draw with Colombia.

In the quarterfinals, the US team faced former coach Pia Sundhage, who was now back with her native Sweden. The US team's offense was relentless, with Morgan and Carli Lloyd spearheading. But the Swedes played a clever defensive game that took the wind out of each successive attacking charge. The Swedes launched into the lead in the 61st minute, when a twenty-year-old defender leaped into a counterattack and fired a shot that caught Hope Solo completely off guard.

The US's attacks grew more ferocious, but the equalizer would have to wait until the 77th minute, when Morgan drilled home a swift shot after the ball had bounced off a Swedish defender. Sweden's defensive play returned to form, however, and the game went into extra time. The outcome would have to be determined through penalty shootout.

The Swedish goalkeeper Hedvig Lindahl saved Morgan's first kick, and Solo then blocked Sweden's third kick. Christen Press took the last kick for the US, and the shot flew over the bar. The USWNT was officially ousted from the Olympics.

## DIGNIFIED IN DEFEAT

It is important that athletes are dignified in their victories as well as their defeats. Hope Solo made disparaging comments about the Swedish team following the USWNT's devastating loss at the Olympics. She drew widespread criticism for her statements, though many—including a few Swedish players—understood her words as having been spoken in the heat of the moment.

Morgan admitted that the defeat was "super heartbreaking," but she said it was nonetheless something that all athletes can expect in their careers, underlining that she in no way agreed with Solo's comments.

## GERMAN GOLD

The Swedes defeated Brazil in the semifinals, after winning another penalty shootout. They then confronted Germany in the final. Germany ended Sweden's streak with a 2–1 victory, and they are therefore the reigning Olympic champions—that is, until the US team takes another shot at the gold during the 2020 Summer Olympics in Tokyo.

## MILESTONES

Morgan played her 100th match for the US national team in a 5–0 friendly win against Ireland on January 23, 2016. The game would see both a goal and an assist from Morgan in a 5–0 US victory.

   In a match against the Costa Ricans at the 2016 CONCACAF Olympic qualifiers, Morgan scored the fastest goal in the tournament's history, and in US soccer history, after only twelve seconds of play. Morgan would add another goal in the game, which also resulted in a 5–0 win for the US.

Alex Morgan collides with Linda Sembrant of Sweden during the women's soccer quarterfinals at the 2016 Olympics.

# ALEX MORGAN, CELEBRITY

Alex Morgan is a superstar in the US and around the world. Her level of fame is best illustrated by how often she has been featured on the covers of the world's most popular magazines.

Alex Morgan at the 2015 ESPY Awards at the Microsoft Theatre LA

# A ROLE MODEL IN THE MOVIES

Morgan's career took a new turn in June 2018, when her first movie was released. In *Alex & Me*, she plays herself as a kind of "invisible friend" to a young soccer player. Siena Agudong plays fourteen-year-old Reagan Willis, who lives for soccer. Reagan idolizes Alex Morgan and a large poster of the soccer legend adorns one wall of her room. However, Reagan fails to make it into her favorite soccer club, and her parents are too focused on her soccer-playing older brother to provide her with the support she needs. As a result, Reagan nearly decides to give up on her soccer dreams, but then Alex Morgan magically steps out from the poster on the wall and offers to help her improve her game. The duo become friends, and through Morgan's dedicated and positive coaching, Reagan gets a second chance to achieve her goal. Her parents finally see the error of their ways and decide to pay more attention to their daughter's soccer passion.

Agudong is an experienced TV actress, but she also plays soccer in real life, and Alex Morgan is one of her favorite players. It was like a dream come true when Morgan was there to give her advice, both in real life and in the movie.

"[Alex] was telling me to have confidence in myself," Agudong said of her incredible experience. "She was really supportive and was always

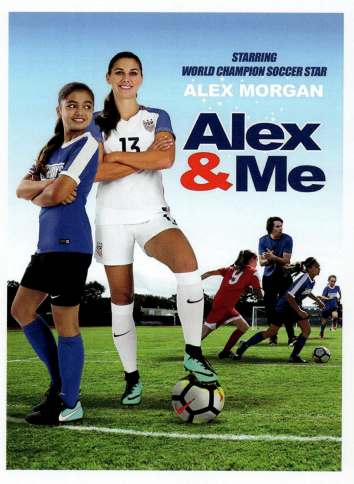

telling me to believe in myself [...] and just do it."

The movie's critical reception was favorable. It was seen as an uplifting tale of how a young person can achieve her goals with passion and drive, and with the support of her family.

# . . . AND IN REAL LIFE

Morgan knows that she is a role model and an inspiration to many young soccer players, and she takes that responsibility very seriously. In early 2019, Morgan unveiled a small soccer field at Vincent Bell Park in Southern California, and then joined a training session with the girls' soccer team from the nearby Glendale High School.

Powerade, the official sports drink of the US women's team, sponsored the field in partnership with the US Soccer Foundation. The US Soccer Foundation seeks to build one thousand soccer fields across the United States by the year 2026, partly with the aim of inspiring young girls to play.

Alex Morgan and actor Siena Agudong attend the premiere of *Alex & Me* at the DGA Theater in Los Angeles, on May 31, 2018.

41

# HER WORLD CUP TEAMMATES

## MEGAN RAPINOE

Rapinoe (b. 1985) brings life to every game she plays in and attracts no less attention off the field through her outspoken political activism. Rapinoe's passes, goal scoring, and inextinguishable fighting spirit are pivotal assets for the national team. Her outstanding performance at the 2019 World Cup earned her the Golden Boot, an award for the tournament's best player.

Megan Rapinoe in action during the 2019 Women's World Cup Group F match against Thailand in Reims, France

Together, Morgan and Rapinoe scored a total of 12 goals in 7 games at the 2019 Women's World Cup tournament. Both also had three assists each.

43

## JULIE ERTZ

Ertz (b. 1992) fit so well into the USWNT when she began playing for the team in 2013 (under her maiden name of Julie Johnston) that it seemed like she had always been there. Ertz is strong and determined, and played as a center back for a while before she changed over to defensive midfielder. She both breaks open the opponent's offense and directs the flow of her team's attacks.

## SAM MEWIS

Not many people were familiar with the powerful midfielder Sam Mewis (b. 1992) before the World Cup in France, but she made her mark on the tournament with her keen eye for passes and assists.

## ROSE LAVELLE

It is no easy task for a newcomer to join such a well-oiled and well-knit team as the USWNT and earn a place in the starting lineup. Lavelle (b. 1995) did precisely that, and she was omnipresent at the 2019 World Cup. This agile attacking midfielder caused a sensation in the center, and her career will no doubt continue to blossom.

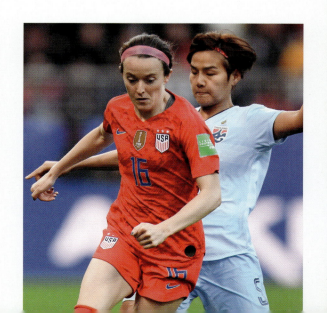

Abby Dahlkemper at the 2019 Women's World Cup final against the Netherlands on July 7, 2019, in Lyon France

Becky Sauerbrunn during the 2019 Women's World Cup final against the Netherlands

## BECKY SAUERBRUNN AND ABBY DAHLKEMPER

The USWNT might have celebrated forwards, but no team becomes world champions without a strong defensive backbone in place. Sauerbrunn (b. 1985) began her career next to the legendary Christie Rampone/Pearce, but lately she has led the US defense like a military commander. She rarely slips up, and she allows the forwards to do what they do best: score goals. Sauerbraunn recently found a worthy partner in Abby Dahlkemper (b. 1993), and together they uphold an unbreakable defensive fortress.

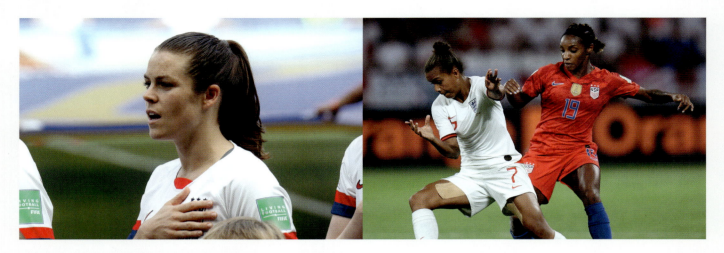

## KELLEY O'HARA AND CRYSTAL DUNN

The American team is known for its attacking wingbacks. O'Hara (b. 1988) is a soccer veteran whose steadfast presence on the right flank is one of the team's most lethal weapons. She is unstoppable. The versatile Crystal Dunn (b. 1992) is younger and even more attack-oriented, racking up goals as a result.

## ALYSSA NAEHER

This stalwart goalkeeper stood for long in the shadow of the colorful and controversial Hope Solo. When the latter retired and had to relinquish her position to an heir, Naeher (b. 1988) stepped up and proved that she was the right woman for the task.

## LINDSEY HORAN

A powerhouse of a midfielder, irreplaceable in both offense and defense, Horan (b. 1994) played for French clubs for four years, which is an unusually long period for a member of the US national team.

## MALLORY PUGH

It can be expected that Pugh (b. 1998), a young and swift forward, will soon team up with Morgan in the frontlines, which speaks volumes about her level of skill.

## CARLI LLOYD

Lloyd (b. 1982) gave an outstanding performance in the 2015 World Cup final that will long be remembered. She was no less a hero at the 2019 tournament in France. She scored 16 goals in 2019, more than any other player that year.

## TOBIN HEATH

Heath (b. 1988) is an attack-oriented midfielder who either sends razor-sharp passes from the right flank or breaks forward to find the back of the net. Heath is not much for the limelight, but she is always on the lookout for clever crosses or goal-scoring chances.

## CHRISTEN PRESS

Press (b. 1988) has been somewhat overshadowed by Morgan and Rapinoe, but she is an excellent shot and lightning quick, and makes clever use of every chance she gets.

# THE 2019 WORLD CUP

## STARTING WITH A BANG

Alex Morgan in action during the 2019 Women's World Cup Group F match against Thailand at Stade Auguste Delaune, Reims, France

The USWNT was the clear fan favorite at the 2019 World Cup in France. But powerful rivals awaited the opportunity to send them packing, and the conclusion of the 2016 Summer Olympics in Rio had shown that the US team was not invincible. However, Team USA proved from the very first game that they were a force to be reckoned with when they utterly demolished Thailand 13—0. Alex Morgan played a leading role in the historic thrashing, scoring a whopping five goals!

## RESPECT

The US team was criticized after the game, in effect for giving it everything they had and celebrating each goal accordingly, even as the lopsided skill level became clear to everyone involved. Morgan and her teammates rejected the criticism. On the contrary, it would have been disrespectful to Thailand if the US had given them an easy pass. The Thai players agreed with the US's response and held their heads high despite their crushing defeat.

## ALEX MORGAN'S GOALS AGAINST THAILAND:

1. Morgan makes a beautiful header on an ingenious cross from Kelley O'Hara.
2. From the flank, Heath directs a header toward the goal. It is intercepted by Morgan, who then flicks the ball into the net with the left foot.
3. Morgan collects the ball near the penalty box, cleverly dribbles past a defender, and blasts a shot straight past the goalkeeper, completing a hat trick.
4. Rapinoe dribbles through the Thai defense and sends a sharp pass to Morgan, who hammers a steady shot into the top corner.
5. Morgan collects the ball outside the box, breaks free of two defenders, sweeps into the box, and nets with a powerful shot.

**Only seven other American soccer players have scored five goals in one game.**
The first was Brandi Chastain, in a game against Mexico during the World Cup qualification tournament in 1991, held in Haiti.

Michelle Akers then scored five goals against Chinese Taipei at the 1991 World Cup in China.

Nine years would pass before the feat was repeated by Tiffany Mibrett, who scored five goals against Panama during the 2002 CONCACAF Gold Cup tournament in Seattle.

Abby Wambach scored her five goals in a friendly game against Panama in 2004.

The 2012 Olympic qualifying tournament in Vancouver took a surprising turn. Amy Rodriguez scored five goals against the Dominican Republic, and Sidney Leroux then went on to score five in a game against Guatemala. Both players had come on as substitutes in the second half.

During the 2016 Olympic qualifying tournament in Frisco, Texas, wingback Crystal Dunn scored five goals against Puerto Rico.

# CHARGING THROUGH THE KNOCKOUT STAGE

Following the victory over Thailand, the games grew increasingly challenging, but there was no stopping Team USA. The offense, led by Morgan, created countless chances. Her scoresheet diminished in the games that followed, because the defenders of opposing teams were busy crowding her; that's when other great US players got the chance to shine.

Chile was easily defeated and even the powerful Swedish team (still led by former USWNT coach Pia Sundhage) failed to hinder the advance of the American juggernaut.

The first opponent in the knockout stage was Spain. The Spanish team put up a good fight but they were ultimately no match for Megan Rapinoe's two penalty kicks. In the quarterfinals, the US squared off with the host team, France. The sturdy yet graceful French team dreamed of taking home a trophy from a major tournament,

but the opportunity slipped away. The American team was simply too powerful for Wendie Renard, Eugenie Le Somner, and their companions. Morgan had faced the French players on various occasions throughout her career, and even played alongside while on loan to Lyon. Rapinoe scored the goals that eliminated the French. She was totally in her element during the tournament.

During this time, Rapinoe was also involved in a social media quarrel with President Donald Trump. Rapinoe is a daring advocate and activist for both LGBTQ and women's rights, as well as an outspoken critic of any form of racism. Morgan, Coach Jill Ellis, and the rest of the team wholeheartedly support Rapinoe's activism and causes.

Soccer was, however, the team's central focus, and now it was time to meet England, a legendary and worthy adversary, in the semifinals.

## FIFA WOMEN'S WORLD CUP 2019

| Date | Place | Opponent | Score | Goal |
|------|-------|----------|-------|------|
| **Group Stage** | | | | |
| 11 June | Reims | Thailand | 13–0 | Morgan 5, Lavelle 2, Horan, Mewis 2, Rapinoe, Pugh, Lloyd |
| 16 June | Paris | Chile | 3–0 | Lloyd 2, Ertz |
| 20 June | Le Havre | Sweden | 2–0 | Horan, 1 own goal |
| **Knockout Stage** | | | | |
| 24 June | Reims | Spain | 2–1 | Rapinoe 2 (penalties)—Hermoso |
| 28 June | Paris | France | 2–1 | Rapinoe 2—Renard |
| 2 July | Lyon | England | 2–1 | Press, Morgan—White |
| 7 July | Lyon | Netherlands | 2–0 | Rapinoe (penalty), Lavelle |

Alex Morgan during the 2019 Women's World Cup semifinal match against England on July 2, 2019, in Lyon, France

51

# THE SEMIFINAL: WHAT A BIRTHDAY!

In order to reach the final, the US first had to face a tough and resilient English team in the presence of 53,000 spectators. For Morgan, the game was particularly significant because it took place on July 2, 2019, her thirtieth birthday.

Rapinoe was injured, so more responsibility fell on Morgan's shoulders than usual. Nevertheless, she and her comrades lived up to the hopes that the American nation had placed in them.

The game started with a bang. Christen Press scored in the 10th minute with a thumping header on Kelley O'Hara's long pass from the flank. The powerful Ellen White leveled the score for the English with a great shot in the 19th minute, and the game became even more intense. Morgan took matters into her own hands after collecting a pass from Lindsey Horan. Despite having an English defender looming over her, she found the back of the net. It was a fabulous goal, and it put the US in the lead. Morgan celebrated her goal by playfully pretending to sip from a teacup. Some criticized Morgan's stunt and claimed it was disrespectful to the English, whose love for tea is well known, but most understood it as simply a good-natured joke from an athlete in her prime.

A long and strenuous battle ensued. The US dominated much of the game, but England snuck in a few dangerous counterattacks. One goal was ruled out for offside, and goalkeeper Naeher decisively stopped a penalty kick toward the end of the game.

England failed to equalize, and captain Alex Morgan led her troops to her third consecutive World Cup final.

---

**ALEX MORGAN ON THE TEA CELEBRATION**

"It wasn't a hit to England in any way. [. . .] I feel that in sport there is a sort of double standard for females in that we have to be humble in our successes and celebrate not too much. You have to laugh about it."

Stefanie van Der Gragt of the Netherlands and Alex Morgan during the 2019 Women's World Cup final in France

## THE RIVALS IN THE FINAL

It was no minor team that awaited the US in the final.

The Dutch team had progressed steadily in recent years and unexpectedly won the UEFA Women's Championship in 2017. The team was therefore a fan favorite at the World Cup in France. They entered the tournament with great confidence and beat Sweden in their semifinal.

The twenty-two-year-old forward Vivianne Miedema counts among the Netherland's most dangerous players, having scored 58 goals in 75 games before the tournament. Miedema plays for Arsenal in England, and she can score goals from anywhere with immense creativity. Another fierce player is the midfielder Lieke Martens, who delivered an outstanding performance at the 2017 UEFA Championship and was named UEFA Women's Player of the Year and FIFA Women's Player of the Year. She is ingenious and attack-oriented, and she easily finishes her attacks with goals.

Then there is the goalkeeper Sari van Veenendaal, whom many consider an even stronger bulwark than the US's goalie Alyssa Naeher.

# THE FINAL

The US won a rather safe victory over a tough Dutch opponent in the 2019 World Cup final. The tournament had attracted vast attention and garnered much enthusiasm from soccer fans around the world. The US and the Netherlands played to an audience of nearly 58,000, among them the king of the Netherlands, Willem-Alexander, and French president Emanuel Macron. The US president failed to show up, but throngs of American soccer fans flocked to the stadium to root passionately for their favorite players. The US team dominated possession in the first half, which came with its fair share of hair-raising attempts. The sturdy Veenendaal just barely managed to save Morgan's shot following a pass from Rapinoe. Morgan returned for another shot, freed herself from the Dutch defenders, and curled a glorious blast from outside the box, but Veenendaal blocked it once again.

The Dutch team played defensively, though with decisive players awaiting chances up front. The stalemate was finally broken in the second half, when a defender took down Morgan in the penalty box. After consulting video replay, the referee awarded the US a penalty shot. Rapinoe stepped to the spot and safely scored her sixth goal of the tournament. With one hand practically clutching the trophy, the promising young player Rose Lavelle cemented the victory eight minutes later by scoring the winning goal after a solo run. The Dutch battled on, but the Americans thwarted their every attempt.

Team USA had earned their fourth—and wholly deserved—World Cup trophy!

## 2019 WORLD CUP FINAL
PARC OLYMPIQUE LYONNAIS, LYON, FRANCE
JULY 7, 2019

## USA – NETHERLANDS
## 2–0

RAPINOE (PENALTY) 61
LAVELLE 69

NAEHER
O'HARA (KRIEGER 46) - DAHLKEMPER - SAUERBRUNN - DUNN
MEWIS - ERTZ - LAVELLE
HEATH (LLOYD 87) - MORGAN - RAPINOE (PRESS 79)

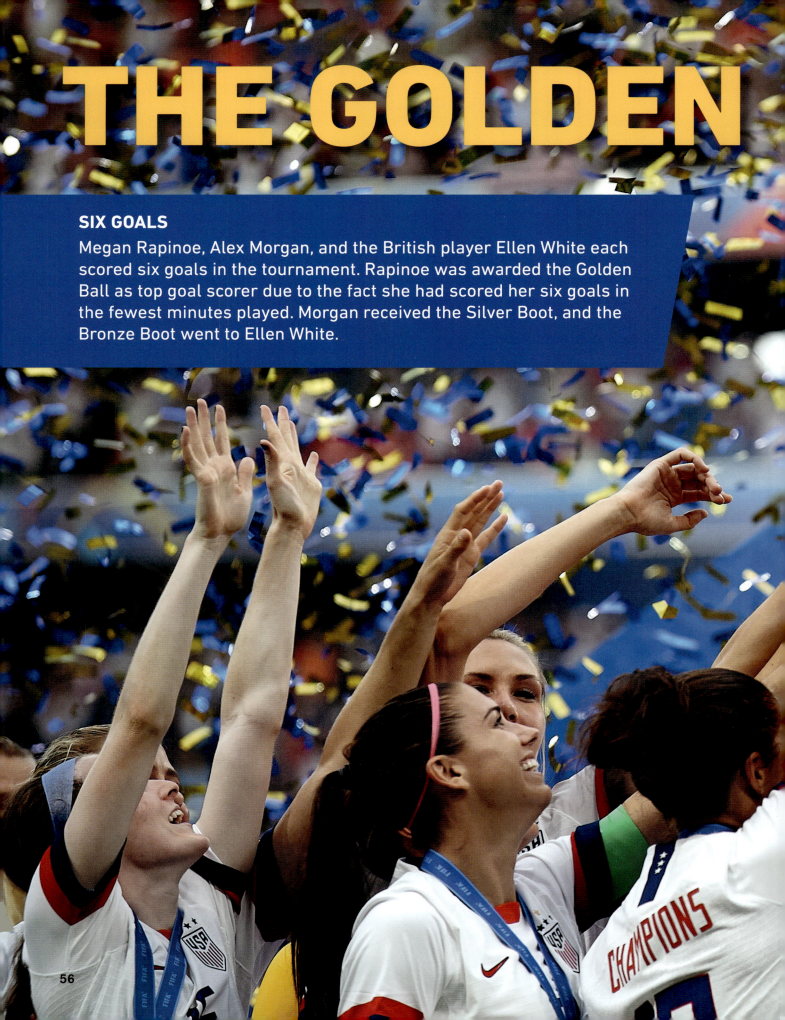

# THE GOLDEN

## SIX GOALS

Megan Rapinoe, Alex Morgan, and the British player Ellen White each scored six goals in the tournament. Rapinoe was awarded the Golden Ball as top goal scorer due to the fact she had scored her six goals in the fewest minutes played. Morgan received the Silver Boot, and the Bronze Boot went to Ellen White.

# MOMENT

| WORLD CUP TITLES | | |
|---|---|---|
| USA | 4 | 1991, 1999, 2015, 2019 |
| Germany | 2 | 2003, 2007 |
| Norway | 1 | 1995 |
| Japan | 1 | 2011 |

**Team USA** celebrates after winning the 2019 Women's World Cup final against the Netherlands on July 7, 2019, at Stade de Lyon in Lyon, France.

Megan Rapinoe and Alex Morgan at the USWNT's victory parade in New York City on July 10, 2019

# "WE'LL CONTINUE TO FIGHT"

The joy after the victory in France reached ecstatic heights. But Morgan and her teammates were nowhere near done. At the ticker-tape parade for the USWNT in New York City, Morgan commented on the status of women players in the soccer world. "We'll continue to fight for what is right and what we deserve and we continue to say the same thing. It's not just about equal pay. It's about equal investment in the sport. It's about equal marketing, advertising and along those lines it's about equal opportunity for us to make similar or the same income as the men's team."

Ongoing success on the field was also a top priority. And the national team continued its victorious stride, beating one challenging opponent after the other, but Alex Morgan was absent from the scoresheet. She was busy preparing for a new chapter in her life.

# "THIS IS CRAZY"

One of Alex Morgan's co-captains, Megan Rapinoe, delivered a powerful speech in New York, and her teammates agreed with every word.

"This is crazy. This is absolutely insane. I'm such at a loss for words. I mean I'll find them, don't worry! But . . . ridiculous. First and foremost, my teammates. [. . .] This group is so resilient, is so tough, has such a sense of humor. . . . There's nothing that can faze this group. We're chillin'. We got tea-sippin', we got celebrations. We have pink hair and purple hair, we have tattoos and dreadlocks. We got white girls and black girls and everything in between. Straight girls and gay girls. I couldn't be more proud to be a co-captain with Carli [Lloyd] and Alex [Morgan] of this team. It's my absolute honor to lead this team out on the field. There's no other place that I would rather be."

# THE FUTURE

In October 2019, Morgan and her husband Servando Carrasco announced that they were expecting their first child, a girl due in April 2020. Her countless fans and social media followers celebrated the news with the happy couple. Some expressed concern that Morgan's pregnancy could possibly prevent her from playing with the USWNT at the 2020 Summer Olympics in Tokyo, Japan. The tournament is set to begin around the middle of July.

Morgan was quick to respond. "It's my goal to play there," she announced. "It's clearly a short window but if I'm able to, I want to be there. "

In an interview with *USA Today*, Morgan added, "There are so many women that have been able to come back to their respective sport after pregnancy and continue to have a successful family while playing their sport that they love at the highest level." She went on, "I plan to follow in those footsteps and be one of those women who have a family and carry my daughter around as I'm going to the next city to play. And I still want to continue to enjoy the sport that I've been playing for all my life."

## CARRASCO

Morgan and Carrasco (b. 1988) married on December 31, 2014. Carrasco began playing soccer at an early age and, like his wife, played for the California Golden Bears at UC Berkeley. He has played with a number of the most powerful teams in US Major League Soccer since then, joining the ranks of the LA Galaxy at the same time as Zlatan Ibrahimovic. Carrasco plays as a defensive midfielder.

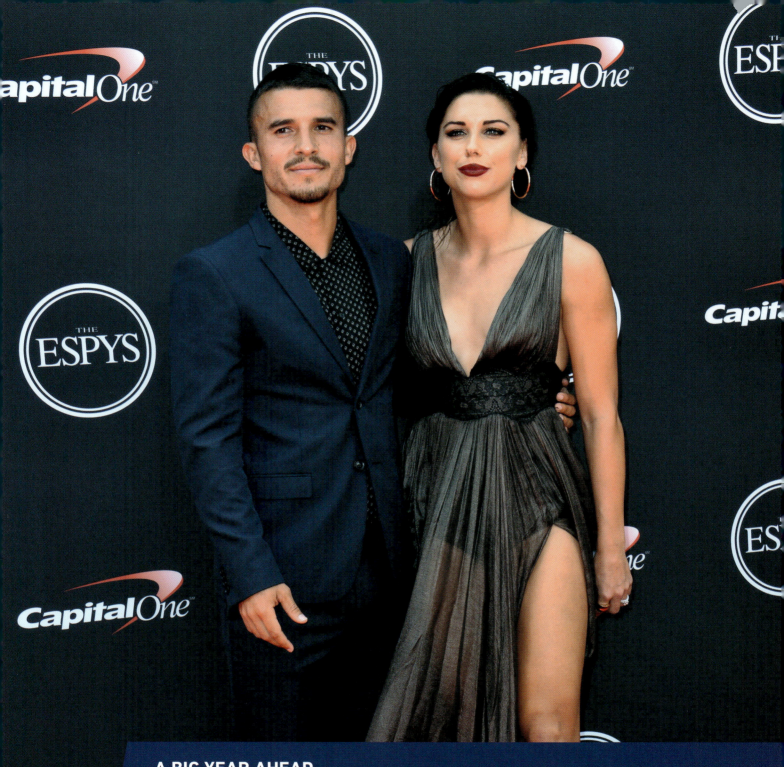

## A BIG YEAR AHEAD

"I have another big year ahead of me and I think whatever I'm planning to do, the plans will probably dissolve," she said. "It always happens where nothing happens according to plan. So I just am taking it week by week, enjoying my time with my husband and my family in the city of L.A. and just eagerly awaiting the arrival of our baby girl."

—Morgan, speaking to *USA Today*'s Josh Peter

**WHAT A MOMENT**

"One of the best moments ever," Morgan said of the ticker-tape parade in New York celebrating the 2019 World Cup win. "Just seeing hundreds of thousands of people come out and support us. Chanting our names, chanting 'Equal Pay,' we've heard a lot of that. And just supporting us was incredible."